BORDERLINE MOTHER

Maternal Psychological Control and Borderline Personality Disorder

© **Written by Dora Dayson**

Contents

Introduction

It is almost a general consensus that childhood is the most careless, most innocent and most cherished part of a human life. People remember their childhood with a smile on their faces, wishing they could get back and appreciate these precious moments of carefree life and innocence. People also tend to forget in this sweet reminiscence that children are actually the most fragile forms of our humanity and if not cherished and looked after, children may suffer long after they seized being children. This is often the case with adults who grew up with a parent or parents suffering from NPD and BPD, which in most cases leaves traumas that influence development of negative qualities such as echoism, depression, anxiety, trust issues, damaging and destructive behavior, self-harm and negative thoughts, negative behavior patterns, problems in relationships and inability to connect and resolve conflicts, and numerous side effects that later on create issues that grow to an emphasis in adulthood and later years in life. To help you understand what you have been through while being raised by NPD or BPD parent from an objective point of you, we decided to create *The Borderline Mother: Growing Up with a Narcissistic Parent with Borderline Disorder guide* and help you come to a resolution of traumas you may be suffering from, all with the goal of living a happy and fulfilling life. You will learn how NPD and BPD acts from a scientific point of view backed by research, but you will also gain access to a variety of helpful techniques that should help you relieve your negative experiences and embrace the fact that your trauma doesn't define who you are. You are the one holding the key to a resolution of your problems, we are only here to help you realize that you can live the life you know you deserve despite bad experiences in your past.

Chapter 1:

What is Borderline Personality Disorder – Defining Borderline Personality Disorder and Narcissism

Borderline Personality Disorder, abbreviated to BPD, is a mental disorder that involves frequent and periodical mood swings, varying image of oneself, as well as frequently changing behavior. People who are suffering from borderline personality disorder are often confused by their own personality, which is marked with uncertainty about who they are and what is their place in the world. Things that are viewed as acceptable by BPD patients at one moment, may trigger anger, irritation, depression and anxiety at another moment. These episodes of emotional outbursts can last from several hours to a couple of days, which usually affects everyone involved and not only the person affected with a borderline personality disorder. Another thing that people with BPD are struggling with is the case of seeing everything as black and white – there are rarely grey areas when they are considering beliefs, perception and other factors they feel affected by. That means that borderline personality disorder goes hand in hand with extremes – BPD changes the perspective without allowing the affected person to consider the fact that nothing is only good or only bad. Furthermore, BPD patients tend to change their beliefs and convictions very often, so not only that they are battling with frequent mood swings, but even their beliefs and opinions can be drastically changed from one day to another. All of these symptoms arrive with increased irritability and confusion, while irritability is often triggered by confusion and even minor factors and situations that wouldn't normally cause extreme emotional outbursts. Even though living with a borderline disorder is difficult, especially in cases where BPD is not treated as a serious mental condition it represents, it may be even more difficult to share your life with a person who is suffering from a borderline personality disorder. There are more than several types of BPD disorders, one of which is narcissistic personality disorder. Children who are raised and are being raised by parents who are suffering from BPD, can develop mental problems themselves, often developing insecurities about who they are themselves. While some children are able to withstand the effects of being raised by a "borderline mother" or a parent suffering from a borderline personality disorder, which represents a small number of cases, other children are deeply affected during their childhood as well as feeling the effects of the way they were brought up later on in adulthood.

Since you are reading this book, the chances are that you have been raised by a parent suffering from a borderline personality disorder. In order to help you cope with the way you were brought up, and potential "damages" that growing up with a borderline mother (or a father) brought upon you, we would first need to present to you what borderline personality disorder represents so that you could also be able to perceive what your parent has been going through, and might still be going through is BDP was left untreated.

Getting back to the way BPD is affecting patients suffering from this type of mental disorder, BPD may also make a person unable to form and maintain meaningful relationships, which consequently affects the relationship between a parent and a child (children). Due to the fact that BPD patients are prone to changing their opinions frequently and rarely based on viable facts, "enemies" may become friends in a blink of an eye, and friends can likewise become enemies. The sense of abandonment and emotional dissatisfaction and emptiness, may drive borderline personality disorder patients to base their relationships based on the need for being loved and also based on the fear of being abandoned. Such behavior may drive BPD patients to become intimate and close to someone they don't even know well, while the other extreme may have them break a long-term relationship with someone without a logical reason. When it comes to logic and deduction, it is very difficult to determine what is "good" or "bad" based on facts as BPD patients are usually focused on how they feel about something or someone based on the moment when they feel intense emotions that are often too intense to cope with. Borderline disorder can be successfully treated and annulated to the point where the patient is able to live a fulfilling and happy life, however, it may be very difficult to convince a BPD patient that they need to seek for help, especially in cases where moods swings and changes in opinion and behavior are too frequent and caused by minor irritations. Eventually, people who are connected to people suffering from borderline personality disorder end up suffering as well. This is especially difficult for children that are unable to perceive that their parent is acting in a certain way because they are affected by a serious mental condition. Ultimately, BPD doesn't only affect the person suffering from this disorder, but also people surrounding that person – friends and family. It may be easy stop being friends with someone who is living with BPD or is treating BPD, as well as divorce or leave someone who is not taking care of BPD as it should – as a serious problem – however, children who are growing up with parents who are suffering from BPD may just be one of the greatest challenges for that child. For children, parents represent the foundation of the family – pillars of the family that are strong and stable – and when these pillars are not holding up and the foundation is weak, the entire family is suffering, while children always get the worst of such cases.

To comprehend what a child may be exposed to on a daily basis when growing up and being brought up by a parent who is suffering from BPD, it is important to get a closer insight into behavior, emotions and cognition of BPD parents, most often the "borderline mother" as children in the early age of growing up are usually the most dependable on their mother, even though the fatherhood role also plays a major role in the way children are brought up.

The feeling of abandonment is strong and intensive with BPD, whether the abandonment case is imagined or in fact real, which means that BPD patients may be obsessing with thoughts of abandonment. They are more likely to do anything and everything once they perceive that there is a chance that someone is about to abandon them. This "chance" doesn't even need to be backed by facts – it can be perceived through distorted perception and false convictions, making the situation harder for all parties involved. In these situations, much like in any other conviction, BPD patients will go to extremes, which means that out of imagined fear of abandonment, BPD patient may be too affectionate or decide to stop communicating with the other person as "prevention", believing that they will be abandoned - most of these impressions are imagined as BPD patients are struggling with distorted cognition.   Another problem that people with borderline personality disorder are experiencing is the case of having a hard time maintaining healthy relationships with friends and family. At one moment, BPD will manifest extreme affection and even idolization of loved ones, which may be followed by a different extreme, which is feeling anger and devaluing loved ones, usually based on minor conflicts that shouldn't cause such extreme reactions. Since the range of emotions BPD patients are experiencing is often too strong to handle, they are more likely to act impulsively and based on what they feel or believe without giving much thought to facts. Borderline personality disorder also facilitates unstable and often dangerous behavior, which may pose as extreme spending, unsafe sex, overeating or even as alcohol or drug addiction. BPD patient will have an unstable and distorted image of themselves as well, at times believing that they are always right and perfect as they are, while in other occasions, BPD patient may resent the image of themselves. Unstable emotions, distorted cognition and often dangerous, impulsive and destructive behavior, will thus prevent BPD patient from leading a happy and fulfilling life. The fact that many BPD patients tend to feel chronic emptiness, is making this condition even worse, not only for the person suffering from borderline personality disorder, but also for the loved ones – friends and family – who decide to stay around, or have no other options but to stay around in case of children.

There are more than several types of borderline personality disorder, one of which might be among the most commonly diagnosed and less commonly treated – narcissistic personality disorder.

Narcissistic Personality Disorder: Defining NPD

Narcissistic personality disorder, or abbreviated NPD, involves a distorted image of oneself, where a person suffering from NPD tends to attach a great importance to their own personality and identity. This disorder can also be recognized due to increased and almost perverted need for attention and admiration, while NPD patients will often display a lack of empathy which makes it difficult for narcissists to connect with people, understand different emotions and develop and maintain meaningful relationships with other people. Beneath the image of inflated importance and need for attention, NPD patient actually has low self-esteem and is insecure, which means that these feelings may be expressed and enticed by a slightest irritation that would provoke a narcissist. Narcissists perceive themselves as increasingly important, while they might feel that not all people deserve to be around them or have their attention, whereas they are worthy of everyone's and anyone's attention. In case they are not treated in accordance with their own image of inflated importance, they are disappointed, unhappy and even angry. The conviction of superiority is also a part of a narcissistic image, where NPD patient believes that they deserve recognition and attention even without achieving something. Everything described as "best" is "made for them", while NPD patient also tends to monopolize conversations with an excessive need to show their superiority in all areas. Although many people may have a difficult time trying to have a relationship with a narcissist, the frequent display of false superiority comes as most harmful for children growing up with a narcissistic parent. If you were raised by a narcissist, you may have a hard time believing in yourself, while you may believe that nothing you do or anything you achieve would be enough. You may catch yourself always trying your best and always tending to excel and be perfect at everything you do, but whatever you achieve won't feel like a success. You are more likely to grow up as a kind, cuddly and obedient child with great grades and be successful at school, however, you may always feel like an underachiever. Even when you are praised by others, a narcissistic parent, often the mother, will annul that praise and "reveal" you as "not good enough". A narcissistic mother will make you feel special at times, but these outbursts of affection would probably be what SHE needs and not what she believes that you need. You may be grounded without any logical reason and prevented from having fun with your friends – a narcissistic parent may even prevent you from having friends: although not directly, your mother may find ways to sabotage your connections with other people, often convincing you that this or that friend is not good enough for you. This may result in having you believe that you are not good enough for anyone and that no one is really good for you, later on in your adult life.

Narcissistic personality disorder also goes with extreme and intense feeling of depression, anger and disappointment in cases when NPD patient believes that their self-perceived greatness is not being honored or recognized. It is often the case that these emotions will turn to intense outbursts of dissatisfaction that may affect people around NPD patients. When a narcissist is happy, everyone must comply and be happy – when a narcissist is sad, everyone must comply and be sad. In one word, perfection can't be criticized and they are perfect, while the world spins around them – this might perfectly describe an unspoken motto of a narcissist. Even if someone was to suggest that a narcissist is suffering from NPD, suggesting that they should seek for help and treat their condition, a narcissist is less likely to comply precisely because the distorted reality that makes them perfect in their own perception. It is not difficult to conclude how difficult and how confusing growing up with a person suffering from NPD or other types of BPD may be.

Chapter 2:

Borderline Personality Disorder Symptoms and Behavior

Anything that a BPD patient does, regardless of how destructive and "wrong" these actions may be, is completely logical and justified to the person suffering from a borderline personality disorder. Even though these behavior patterns are usually destructive and self-destructive, the distorted cognition and unreal perception would make BPD symptoms into logical responses in the eyes of the person suffering from BPD. In the sense of further defining BPD and what this condition represents, as well as how BPD is displayed and showcased, we are set to present all symptoms that usually define borderline personality disorder, as well as list the types of BPD.

Borderline Personality Disorder Behavior and Symptoms

The following symptoms usually define borderline personality disorder in general. The lack of some symptoms or an isolated presence of certain symptoms doesn't necessarily present a valid diagnosis of BPD.

- *Distorted self-image*

People who are suffering from BPD have a distorted image of themselves. They rely on the way they feel in order to form and develop their emotional reactions, which are often intense, inappropriate in oppose to situations they are in, as well as extreme. BPD patient may perceive their own self as always right and on point at one moment, heavily criticizing and devaluing themselves right afterward. Distorted self-image goes hand in hand with confusion and unstable perception of one's identity and role in this world. This case is not only difficult for the person suffering from BPD, but also for people around them who are left to deal with side-effects of distorted perception.

- *Distorted cognition*

Aside from dealing with distorted self-image, one of the symptoms describing BPD is distorted cognition. Due to distorted cognition, the way BPD patients conclude, deduct and perceive different experiences is actually removing strings that tie a person to reality and facts. BPD patients are less likely to consider viable facts as the truth about reality, and are set to form their perception of reality based on how they feel, which is how emotional responses and behavior are formed as well. BPD patients might believe that their actions and reactions are normal and appropriate, but in reality, they are only harming themselves, usually by failing to maintain functional and meaningful relationships with other people.

- *Impulsive emotional reactions*

Emotional reactions are very intense and almost unable to be contained, which is why BPD patients are less likely to stop and reflect on the way they feel before they decide to react. Due to intensity of emotions, BPD patients are often unable to prevent themselves from having emotional outbursts and impulsive reactions, reacting intensively and inappropriately while the slightest irritation may cause intense emotional reactions. Intense emotional reactions may range from extreme feeling of happiness to intensive feeling of anger, or sadness.

- *Destructive and impulsive behavior*

Distorted cognition and intense emotions go hand in hand with destructive and impulsive behavior. BPD patient may not be able to control the way they react, while these reactions and emotional outbursts combined create destructive and impulsive behavior patterns. BPD patients may display and showcase harmful and risky behavior, which may involve purposefully and intentionally breaking relationships with no viable reasons, reckless driving, overeating, addiction to drugs and alcohol, extreme and uncontrolled spending, as well as self-harming. When in emotional distress, a BPD patient won't stop to reconsider their options and come up with a constructive way to resolve issues, but will react based on impulse, adopted destructive behavior, and intense emotions they see as truth instead of relying on facts.

- *Unstable and dysfunctional perception*

Unstable and dysfunctional perception of experiences and reality is another one of symptoms that may indicate that a person is suffering from BPD. Instability is reflected in constant changing of plans, opinions, beliefs and convictions, which altogether adds to the overall dysfunctionality. Distorted perception itself may affect the quality of life as it may give birth to unstable emotions and dysfunctional behaviors, usually in domain of maintaining relationships with other people. Dysfunctionality may be displayed in both professional and personal life.

- *Extreme emotional reactions*

Extremes are somewhat symptoms that best describe borderline personality disorder, as patients often go from one extreme to another when it comes to forming emotional reactions, opinions and behavior. When it comes to extreme emotional reactions, patients may go from sad to happy and vice versa in a blink of an eye, while emotional reactions that go to extremes may last from few hours to several days. Even though BPD patient would perceive their own reactions as appropriate, these emotional reactions are actually an exaggerated version of appropriate reactions where these emotions are usually triggered by a minor change or a factor of irritation that appears to be insignificant. A mild provocation is enough to ignite extreme emotional reactions. Instead of taking a moment to reflect on what would be the best reaction based on facts and reality, BPD patient will react based on intensity of their own emotions.

- *Mood swings*

Mood swings represent one of the main symptoms that may indicate that a person is suffering from a borderline personality disorder. What may appear as changing moods "out of the blue", actually makes a perfect sense for a person suffering from BPD. Strong and intense emotions may change as fast as the changing opinions and beliefs, which may display in form of mood swings that change periodically and last from a few hours to several days.

- *Changing opinions and beliefs*

Those who are perceived as enemies today may become friends already tomorrow, and those who were viewed as friends may find detest and resent in the matter of a single day. BPD patients are prone to changing beliefs and opinions, being confused themselves on the matter of who they are and what to believe in. Intense emotions are usually the factor of determination for BPD patients, and their opinions and reactions may depend on their mood and how they feel, which may create very unpredictable outcomes and reactions.

- *Feeling of anxiety and depression*

Feeling of anxiety and depression often appear at patients who are suffering from borderline personality disorder often due to the stress caused by fear of abandonment, lack of trust and frequent mood swings. Since the fear and sadness may stick with BPD patients for days, these feelings may easily transform to depression and anxiety as multiplied emotions of sadness and fear.

- *Hostility and increased irritability*

Hostility and increased irritability are frequently present whereas a person suffering from BPD may express hostility towards everything and everyone when it appears that there are no factors that would trigger this sort of behavior. Even the slightest factor viewed as disturbance may trigger irritation, which further results in hostility, intense emotions and impulsive behavior.

- *Trust issues*

Since opinions and beliefs are under constant changing, it is difficult for a BPD patient to determine whom to trust and where not to invest their trust, which eventually ends up with developing trust issues. When changes of opinions and beliefs ensue, trust may switch without a logical reason, while BPD patient will often doubt everyone and anyone's intentions believing that there are hidden motives behind every person's intentions. Trust issues are worsened with increased feeling of anxiety and mood swings.

- *Fear of abandonment*

Fear of abandonment is almost perpetually present, where BPD patients believe that everyone they care for will eventually end up leaving them. Whether the fear is based on facts, or imagined and based on distorted beliefs, the patient will have the feeling that they must do something to prevent abandonment. Here is where tendency towards extremes comes to the surface as BPD patients may either act and react with an increased level of affection, or cut off their communication out of fear of being abandoned and wanting to be the first to abandon. However, often it is the case when it comes to BPD that the fear of abandonment is not justified.

- *Suicidal thoughts and thoughts of self-harm*

As well as it is the case with depressive disorders and anxiety, BPD patients are often driven to suicidal thoughts and thoughts of self-harm, which usually comes as a consequence of intense emotions and other symptoms combined to create an atmosphere of perpetual sadness and doom. If BPD is not treated in accordance with patient's needs, the patient may eventually give into self-harm.

- *Problem with controlling emotions*

We all get upset, stressed out, sad, and angry, and we are all capable of feeling intense emotions.

However, when we are faced to intense emotions, a natural response would be to think through our reactions and actions – otherwise, things may only get worse. When it comes to people affected by BPD, there is no contemplating or thinking through – reactions are almost instant and emotional outbursts are intense and uncontrolled. It is very difficult for a BPD patient to control their emotions, thus making it difficult to find an appropriate reaction in emotionally stressful situations. The overall intensity of emotions is so high that a person is unable to control emotional outbursts. This behavior may not only make things worse for the BPD patient, but it also affects other people involved.

Types of Borderline Personality Disorders

Although borderline personality disorder has been successfully treated for decades now, there are no officially determined schemes that would closely define different types of borderline personality disorders. Given the fact that not all patients suffering from BPD are suffering from the same symptoms, there is a need for forming and defining BPD subtypes, which is how there are two ways of differentiating borderline personality disorders. The following subtypes of BPD represent a scheme created by an American psychologist, Theodore Millon.

- *Impulsive borderline disorder*

According to Millon's categorization and definition of BPD subtypes, people who are suffering from impulsive borderline disorder are usually energetic and generally in a good mood, so people like to be around them. However, when they feel they have been let down, patients with impulsive BPD will explicitly show intense anger and more often act in impulse. Although energetic and talkative, patients with impulsive BPD disorder have a tendency towards controlling social situations and the way their social interactions are being conducted. To remain in the center of attention, a person with impulsive borderline disorder may get involved in risky and dangerous situations, which may cause injuries and leave serious consequences.

- *Discouraged borderline disorder*

People with discouraged borderline disorder appear dependent and needy, and are in constant search for acceptance and approval. Their need for being accepted and getting help they need may drive them to self-harm, which is usually a way of getting what they need – attention from others and the image of a victim. Deep within, although people with BPD are showcasing their need for dependency, approval and acceptance, they are nurturing anger due to the feeling of inferiority, while often perceiving themselves as inadequate. The feeling of inadequacy and inferiority

- *Self-destructive borderline disorder*

As the name of this subtype may suggest itself, self-destructive borderline disorder involves self-destructive behavior, which includes self-harm and any type of dangerous behavior. People suffering from self-destructive disorder are more likely to feel intense anger, dissatisfaction, bitterness and are prone to mood swings. People suffering from this type of BPD usually struggle with the image they have of themselves, also struggling with unfulfilled, repressed and unconscious desires that may drive them to emotional outbursts and impulsive behavior. Even when they are aware of their own desires, they may have a difficult time acknowledging these desires. Moreover, patients with self-destructive BPD tend to work against themselves as a part of self-destructiveness, often sabotaging their own chances of succeeding.

- *Petulant borderline disorder*

Petulant borderline personality disorder involves increased irritability, frustration, anger, and unpredictable behavior in general. People suffering from this type of BPD are often difficult to please as they get easily irritated and have no patience with other people. It may be very easy to trigger irritation, anger and frustration, as people with petulant BPD are easily disillusioned. Moreover, characteristics that usually describe people with this type of BPD are stubbornness, willfulness, defiance and tendency towards passive-aggressive behavior. Patients who are suffering from petulant BPD also have a difficult time admitting they are wrong, which makes it rather hard to maintain relationships and form connections with other people. Instead of resolving a problem based on facts, people with petulant BPD are more likely to act impulsively and based on their own belief that they can't be wrong.

Aside from Theodore Millon's subtypes of borderline personality disorder, there is another way of forming and defining different types of borderline disorders. The following definitions of BPD subtypes were formed in 2017 based on cluster research which included studying severity of symptoms, a total number of symptoms that describe BPD, issues in relationships, personality, functionality, attachment and level of attachment, life considerations and its quality, as well as potential exposure to traumatic experiences and events. Based on all these factors, the following BPD subtypes were formed and defined.

- *Core BPD*

Core BPD is defined as a common, or classic, form of borderline personality disorder and involves most commonly noted symptoms that define BPD in its core. People with core borderline disorder are suffering from well-known symptoms of BPD such as frequent mood swings, distorted self-image and confusion regarding self, unstable behavior and inability to control emotions and prevent emotional outbursts. Anxiety and depression go hand in hand with core BPD, making it even harder for patients suffering from other BPD symptoms. Not only that patients diagnosed with core BPD are suffering from symptoms that describe BPD, but are also experiencing these symptoms more intensely, which adds up to the severity of this type of disorder. Core BPD patients have a great need for intimacy with a tendency towards becoming dependent in relationships – however, the fear of abandonment and other consequences that may arise from becoming intimate with another person, is often preventing core BPD patients from forming and maintaining meaningful relationships. Patients will also go to extremes in order to put their fear of abandonment and neediness at ease, which means that at one moment they will try to please people they want to stay around and at times this affection may easily turn into intrusiveness and neediness. The researchers suggest that core BPD is usually tied to genetic predispositions rather than traumatic experiences.

- *Paranoid/Schizotypal*

Schizotypal or paranoid borderline personality disorder resembles psychosis as people suffering from this type of BPD are usually disconnected from reality and their perception of what reality represents is distorted. Alongside with other BPD symptoms, patients with paranoid BPD tend to isolate themselves, lack assertiveness and may appear as needy due to their expressive need for closeness and intimacy. In case people with this type of disorder feel threatened in any way, they are more likely to retreat in their own world – the fact that these patients are disconnected from reality usually doesn't prevent them from functioning. The lack of confidence is highly present and easily noted, while people with this type of BPD are also agreeable and accommodating when it comes to maintaining relationships with other people. Other people may find their neediness perhaps overwhelming.

- *Externalizing/Extravert*

Even though the researches managed to prove that borderline personality disorders usually depend on genetic predispositions, people with externalizing/extravert BPD are said to have been influenced towards developing this condition due to exposure to traumatic experiences. Aside from experiencing majority of symptoms that describe core BPD, people with extravert BPD are also narcissistic and antisocial. While self-centered and concerned only about their own self, patients suffering from this type of disorder tend to avoid intimacy and connection with other people. They are dominant, tend to criticize others without perceiving their own flaws and mistakes as such, also externalizing their own problem in the sense of looking for guilt in others, the world, society – anyone and anything is rather blamed for experiences that are viewed upon as bad, as they are less likely to accept responsibility for their own decisions and actions. Based on extensive researching concluded in 2017, it has been noted that men are overly presented in this type of BPD, where the condition is usually developed as a consequence of external environmental factors and traumatic experiences.

Even though extravert/externalizing borderline personality borderline disorder has characteristics of narcissism, narcissistic personality disorder is a separately defined condition that likewise involves distorted cognition and lack of empathy for others. In the next chapter, we will define the narcissistic disorder through characteristic symptoms and behavior.

Chapter 3:

Narcissistic Personality Disorder Symptoms and Behavior

Although narcissistic personality disorder has some similarities with borderline personality disorder, narcissism is not the same thing as BPD. BPD type extrovert/externalizing borderline disorder may also resemble narcissistic personality disorder, however, there are specific symptoms that define narcissism as a completely different personality disorder. Some symptoms and behaviors, such as need for attention, issues with maintaining relationships, vulnerable self-esteem and distorted reality and cognition are shared by NPD and BPD. Moreover, people suffering from narcissistic personality disorder have a sense of inflated importance, believing that they deserve attention, admiration and acceptance even in cases where no achievements are made. In order to be able to define narcissistic personality disorder and describe people who are suffering from this condition, the following symptoms are used for diagnosis and determination of general severity of this condition.

Narcissistic Personality Disorder Symptoms and Behavior

Narcissistic behavior often makes up for a negative factor when it comes to relationship development, social interactions and maintaining and forming meaningful relationships. The person suffering from this type of disorder may also lack empathy, thus having a hard time understanding how other people feel. Even in cases where empathy is present and noted, a narcissistic person is more likely to place their own needs as a top priority. Despite visibly high self-esteem, a narcissistic person hides their own insecurities and low self-confidence. The following symptoms define narcissistic personality disorder.

- *Sense of high self-importance*

Not only that people suffering from narcissistic personality disorder tend to display their sense of high self-importance, but they also feel like they matter more in oppose to other people. Moreover, narcissists believe that their company needs to be earned, searching for "likewise important" people. Everything that they own or have is described as "best" as they perceive themselves as important even though they may not have actual achievements that could describe a narcissistic person as "important". Due to their sense of high self-importance, narcissists don't take criticism very well, and believe they deserve special treatment.

- *Sense of entitlement and need for admiration*

One of the greatest wishes that a narcissist may have is to be the center of admiration, and generally the center of everything as they may perceive that the world is spinning around them in connection with their sense of high self-importance. Sense of entitlement is present even though their achievements don't match their perception of self-importance. In case a narcissist doesn't get what he wants, irritation may be triggered as a consequence and impulse reactions may follow as it is the case with borderline personality disorder and inability to control emotions in stressful situations.

- *Exaggerating*

Exaggeration is an overly present symptoms as narcissists tend to inflate their importance, achievements, and talents, all with the goal to feel as if they are better than other people – entitled. Exaggeration may also appear in form of impulse reactions and in cases of criticizing others where a narcissistic person will exaggerate in describing other people's flaws and lack of importance, while they may compare themselves with other people in the sense of demining achievements of others.

- *Disillusion about perfection*

Narcissists are also coping with disillusion about perfection, believing that they deserve a perfect job, house, partner, romantic relationship – everything. A person suffering from narcissistic personality disorder craves for a special treatment which matches their idea of perfection, failing to realize that nothing is truly perfect.

- *Lack of empathy*

Lack of empathy or inability to respond to empathy is another one of symptoms that describe narcissistic personality disorder. People who are suffering from NPD have a difficult time connecting with other people due to their inability to feel what others feel. Even in cases where a narcissist is able to recognize needs of other people, NPD will make them "immune" to providing a suitable reaction unless necessary for adding up to their self-image of superiority.

- *Conviction of superiority*

A narcissist believes that they can do better than others, while thinking they own an unfillable ability to excel in anything and everything. The feeling of superiority makes them believe they are better in oppose to others, which again makes it difficult for a narcissist to form meaningful connections with other people. Moreover, their conviction of superiority prevents them from recognizing their own mistakes and encouraging conviction that they are not capable of committing errors.

- *Envious and anxious*

As a part of low self-esteem as a perfect opposition of displayed high self-esteem, narcissists often feel intense envy and anxiety. Deep below, they are aware of the fact that there are people who are in some ways and in many ways better than them, which causes anxiety alongside envy and jealousy.

- *Low self-esteem*

Low self-esteem remains hidden and in the shadow of openly showcased high self-esteem, which represents extremes similar to behavior present in BPD. Instead of working on improving themselves and work on their self-esteem through affirmations and talk therapies, narcissists are more likely to ignore the fact that they have issues as that would jeopardize the image of perfection and superiority they are using to convince others and themselves into their own perception of entitlement in search for admiration and attention.

- *Seemingly high self-esteem*

Openly displaying high self-esteem through narcissistic behavior, the image of high self-esteem and high confidence is one of the key characteristics of people suffering from NPD. High self-esteem always goes hand in hand with low self-esteem in case of narcissistic personality disorder. While displaying high self-esteem, the person suffering from NPD will at the same time feel the lack of confidence experienced through low self-esteem. Secretly coping with low self-esteem, a narcissist is likely to develop envy and jealousy towards people who appear better than themselves in any way. The fact that there is someone who can "compete" with them may appear as a threat and may cause increased irritability.

- *Unwilling to recognize other people's needs*

Even though narcissists may be able to note other people's emotions and needs, they are rather unwilling to recognize other people's needs. Empathy may be present; however, a narcissist is less likely to act upon other people's needs, considering that their needs must always come first. This case may be connected to the feeling of entitlement that usually marks narcissistic disorder.

- *Inability to recognize other people's needs*

Aside unwillingness to recognize other people's needs, narcissists may also be unable to recognize other people's needs and emotions. The difference between the two is undoubtedly the lack of empathy, which furthermore decreases the chances forming and developing meaningful connections with other people. Having a relationship is difficult when the lack of empathy gets in the way of communicating.

- *Arrogant and pretentious behavior*

Arrogance and pretentious behavior is one of the key behaviors expressed by a narcissist. Distorted cognition creates a conviction that narcissists are better than others, which is why they act with arrogance, boastfulness and pretentious behavior. This type of behavior usually ruins any chances for forming and developing connections with others.

- *Distorted cognition/reality*

Distorted cognition/reality affects the way narcissists are thinking, but it also defines the way they behave and act upon how they feel. Distorted reality includes the sense of superiority, the sense of entitlement, imagined high self-esteem, and imagined importance without necessarily having achievements.

Chapter 4:

Differences Between Borderline Personality Disorder and Narcissistic Disorder

Borderline personality disorder and narcissistic disorder are different types of disorders in many ways, which is displayed through behavior and symptoms that define the two mental problems. Even though some symptoms and behaviors may overlap and match, NPD and BPD represent different types of mental issues, both for people who are suffering from these conditions and people around them. Before we move onto analyzing what it is like to grow up with a borderline mother and/or narcissistic parent, we will first discuss differences between borderline personality disorder and narcissistic disorder. By listing differences in symptoms and behavior, diagnosing a mental condition and recognizing the exact problem becomes significantly easier.

NPD and BPD: Differences vs Similarities

While narcissistic personality disorder and BPD may have a lot of similarities when it comes to symptoms and some forms of behavior, triggers and causes behind these symptoms are fairly different, which is how the two can be separately defined and differentiated. NPD and BPD might actually represent opposites in some cases. For example, a narcissistic person has a well-defined feeling of entitlement and superiority, while a person suffering from borderline personality disorder usually believes that there is something awfully wrong with them, which more likely causes a retreat and introvert behavior. Majority of narcissists are expressing extravert behavior, while many types of borderline PD will be marked with introvert behavior with extravert BPD as an exception. Another case that clearly showcases the difference between BPD and NPD is the fact that people who are suffering from BPD are prone to idealization as well as devaluation of people. In case of NPD, a constant devaluation of other people's abilities, characteristics, behaviors and achievements are devalued. While NPD patients are convinced that they deserve the best, relatable to the sense of entitlement, BPD patients are more likely to believe that they are worthless, while also being inclined towards self-criticism. While differences are clearly able to help us set apart BPD from NPD and recognize each of these conditions, similarities can make determination of each condition more complex. However, even these similarities can serve in favor of specific determination as factors and triggers that define these similar symptoms are different in both conditions. For instance, one of noted similarities in symptoms shared by NPD and BPD patients is seen in increased need for attention. Both, NPD and BPD patients have increased need for attention as one of the noted symptoms which help defined these conditions. In case of BPD patients, the need for attention will be triggered as a symptom due to the fear of abandonment that people with BPD usually have. They can be perceived as needy and clingy as they are having a hard time balancing their need for attention. This need will be displayed through extremes, where the person suffering from BPD might either cut communication with the other party or become too affectionate to the point where the other person might feel suffocated. The need for attention in case of a person suffering from NPD will be entirely different as this need will be aggressively displayed not because of the fear of abandonment but because of sense of entitlement and superiority, which makes it easier for them to become the one abandoning in oppose to fearing abandonment – as noted in comparison of two opposite motives standing behind the same symptom, it becomes obvious that even similarities when closely analyzed and observed may help differentiate NPD from BPD. Another similarity that might make it more difficult to set NPD apart from BPD is the case of moodiness and impulsive reactions and behavior. Both, NPD and BPD patients will express moodiness and act and behave impulsively in accordance with the way they feel – once again, the only difference between the two when faced to these similarities lies in the motive behind these symptoms. Moodiness at NPD patients will usually appear when they fail to get what they want, considering that they deserve the best, as well as in case of lacking expected attention from others. People suffering from NPD will also act impulsively when something falls out of the vision they have on what they deserve and what they should get. On the other hand, moodiness at BPD patients arrives with frequent mood changes, which is one of the most commonly noted symptoms in borderline personality disorder. Impulsive behavior will appear as a result of inability to control; strong emotions they have as the result of confusion as while NPD patients have a distorted image of high self-importance, BPD patients are often confused about who they are frequently changing opinions, believes, and convictions as a part of their condition. Both can be easily agitated; however, agitation will come with different triggers. In case of BPD, agitation may arrive with changes that are not well accepted, distorted cognition that drives BPD patients to extremes, while agitation may be even triggered with the changing seasons or experiences they perceive as stressful. All of these differences and similarities may help you determine what you are facing, or what you have been faced to during your childhood, which might have defined some of your actions, behavior, emotions and thoughts later on in your life. To help you gain a better understanding of what you have been going through during the period of your bringing up, we will present you with an objective overview of how a life with NPD and BPD parent might look like, or might have looked like in your specific case. Before we proceed to the next chapter where you will be able to learn more details on what it appears to be growing up with a borderline mother, we are going to list differences and similarities recorded in cases of narcissistic personality disorder and borderline personality disorder.

Similarities Between Narcissistic Personality Disorder and Borderline Personality Disorder

- **_Insecurity_** – although it may appear that NPD patients are not displaying insecurity as a true opposition to their presentation of high self-confidence, people suffering from NPD are insecure deep within, which leads to resent towards other people, jealousy, envy and open devaluation of other people. In case of BPD patients, insecurity will be showcased through distorted thoughts and cognition which makes them doubt themselves and who they actually are. The fear of abandonment is another form of insecurity noted in behavior of BPD patients.

- *Overwhelming emotions* – this symptom appears in both cases, while both profiles will also act upon their feelings by developing impulsive reactions and behavior. Whichever emotion they are experiencing, NPD and BPD patients will feel it with increased intensity, which usually leads to impulsive reactions.

- *Destructive and unstable relationships* – due to the fact that NPD and BPD patients are coping with intense emotions that are difficult to stabilize and tame to the point where considering a non-impulsive reaction is possible before forming patterns of destructive behavior. Destructive behavior and inability to hold back from reacting impulsively is what leads to unstable and destructive relationships in both cases – NPD and BPD.

- ***Interpersonal challenges*** – doubts, fears, insecurity, anxiety and even depression, may easily become a part of everyday life of people suffering from NPD and BPD, posing as interpersonal challenges that need to be overcome. While it may be difficult to overcome fear of abandonment in case of BPD or sense of entitlement and superiority in case of NPD, becoming aware of interpersonal challenges and realizing that there is an actual problem in cognition and behavior, may bring NPD and BPD patients closest to a viable solution that would help them treat their condition in a successful way. Due to interpersonal challenges, NPD and BPD patients often have a difficult time keeping a job or maintaining a meaningful relationship.
- ***Isolation*** – despite the fact that people who are suffering from NPD feel entitled to "best" while having increased need for attention, they can still retreat to isolation, both physically and socially. NPD patients may be driven to isolation in cases where they feel like they are not

getting enough attention or that their imagined supremacy is not taken seriously which often happens. BPD patients may isolate as well, however, their motive would be different than the one noted in case of NPD – BPD patient may retreat to avoid irritation triggers. Moreover, people suffering from BPD often doubt themselves, have low self-esteem and are confused about their own identity, which is why they tend to retreat to isolation as well.

- *Fear* - both types of patients are prone to anxiety and panic attacks, which appears as a result of living in fear. Some people may obsess with their own fears, and some may fear periodically or occasionally, however, in either case the fear is intense and can also be paralyzing for the patient. The most commonly noted fear at patients with BPD is fear of abandonment and fear of being let down and betrayed. Narcissists may fear that they will never be able to find their equal, considering themselves to be superior.

- *Distorted cognition* – Distorted cognition is present in both cases and is considered to be the main trigger of previously listed symptoms and types of behavior noted at NPD and BPD patients. Distorted cognition also makes patients believe that their perception is the true image of reality, which further makes it difficult for NPD and BPD patients to seek for help. Seeking for help and admitting that something is wrong would be especially difficult for someone who is suffering from NPD due to the false image of perfection, impeccability and supremacy.

To face what you have been through as a child growing up with a parent who is suffering from either narcissistic personality disorder or borderline personality disorder, or even both, which is possible in some cases, we will move onto the next chapter and discuss about being brought up by a borderline mother, i.e. a parent suffering from borderline disorder.

Chapter 5:

Growing Up with a Borderline Mother: BPD Parenting

Some children tend to blame themselves for the ways they have been mistreated or neglected while growing up, which often happens in dysfunctional families where bringing up children is not set in the first plan and creating a healthy environment for a child is not an option. There are many factors that can trigger dysfunctions within families, one of them being a parent with a mental condition that needs to be treated but is often not considered as a problem by the patient. For children before the age of adolescence where4 children tend to look for role models outside the family life, parents are the first and most important role models. In many ways, sometimes regardless of characteristics of the child, parents are playing a major role in forming their children's identity. Children look up to their parents as they share living space and more importantly, they share a family. Children will learn how to read and how to use a toothbrush and tie shoelaces, all from their parents, but children also observe how their parents behave, reacting and acting in accordance with behavioral patterns displayed by parents. We can start from the most trivial example and mention how children learn to say "Thank you" and "Goodbye" when appropriate, while also mentioning how some children might be bullying other children just because they noted aggressive behavior in their parents' behavior. However, sometimes, children can display aggressive behavior even when growing up in healthy conditions, which is why the previous example shouldn't be consider as inclusively limited to wrong models as the main cause. Based on child's character, a narcissistic parent may help raise a narcissistic child as children tend to adopt the way their parents behave if inclined towards such behavior through personal characteristics and identity potential. More commonly, a narcissistic parent will create an insecure child with low self-esteem and potential of developing condition such as depression and anxiety. Children are more likely to blame themselves for suffering brought by their parents while trusting perception their parents are forcing on them. When it comes to growing up with a parent suffering from borderline personality disorder, most commonly borderline mother, children are also prone to developing a personality disorder themselves or develop a different condition due to traumatic experiences during childhood and early adolescence. Most commonly, children who have grown up with a parent suffering from a borderline disorder are prone to depression, anxiety disorder, and are more likely to express antisocial and introvert behavior. Some children tend to avoid remembering traumatic experiences that took place in their childhood, which may lead to avoiding situations that resemble these traumas in any way. To get a closer insight into what being brought up by a borderline mother looks like, and to help you identify your own experiences through our universal guidance, we are going to analyze influences, parent-child relationship, as well as development affected by growing up with borderline mother.

How Growing Up with a Borderline Mother Influences the Child in Infancy Stage

Children are born with the need to be loved, nurtured and accepted, while it is often the idea that childhood is the most innocent period in everyone's life. The part that involves innocence in being brought up, however, is not always present, especially in cases when children are growing up in dysfunctional families. In these cases, childhood of the affected child is losing its innocence as children are in fact the most vulnerable units of family as a whole and seek for protection and support. Children who are born to and raised by borderline mothers are usually affected already in earliest days of infancy, when connection with mother is the most important thing for infant's development. Infants seek for attachment, security and engagement, while infants feel most secure when beside their mothers, which is only natural. Infants react to their mother's smell, emotions, voice, presence and even the sound of her heartbeat as the most familiar things which helps them identify security. Mother's presence can calm down an infant and convince it into feeling secure and safe. Borderline mothers tend to fail in responding to their infant's needs and are often insensitive to infant's distress. Borderline mothers may feel like their child in its infancy stage is intruding her life and preventing her from being happy. Sometimes, these symptoms are the exact keys for identification of "baby blues", i.e. depression that often appears after pregnancy. However, borderline mothers will have a constant feeling of intrusion and are less likely to provide a suitable response when their baby is in distress and needs them despite realizing this case as a fact. As infants are developing and growing up, the need for attention surpasses feeding, sleeping and changing diapers, which leads to parent-child activities that involves playing with the baby, touching it, smiling at the baby and observing how baby is reacting to mother's voice, presence and face. Mothers who are suffering from BPD are less likely to smile at their baby, play with the infant and connect through touch, sounds and facial expressions. Furthermore, borderline mothers are less likely to come up with an appropriate response to the emotional state of their children, which affects infants starting from the earliest period of their childhood. Due to negative psychological and social behavior displayed by borderline mothers, children can feel insecurity, discomfort, and develop a sense of disassociation from the early start of their childhood, which also represents a critical point of childhood development. Despite the absence of vocal communication in this stage of childhood, babies still require appropriate response, vocalization and expression of attachment, i.e. using touch to connect with the infant – even though an infant is unable to understand and process complex relations and their own needs that come in form of inborn necessity, negative responses such as those noted at borderline mothers, may influence the infant in a negative way and condition the further development of the child.

Verbal Stage: Borderline Mother Effects on the Verbal Stage of Childhood

Parents are not only caretakers and role models to their children – children also look up to their parents while forming the way they perceive others, the world around them and themselves, which further helps them define their own identity. The effects of a borderline parenthood become even more obvious in the verbal stage of a child's life as children are learning how to respond, behave, act and react to internal and external factors. The fact that a borderline mother is expressing fear of abandonment, distorted perception of reality and the world, black and white perspective which nurtures extremes, impulsive behavior and inability to recognize her child's needs may deeply affect the overall development of that child, affecting its development psychologically and socially. Children being brought up by borderline mothers are less likely to be praised and gain recognition, as borderline mothers will have a difficult time coming up with appropriate emotional responses due to the lack of empathy, compassion and are prone to impulsive and extreme behavior. The fact that a BPD mother may be happy at one moment and then angry and furious in the next second may make the child feel insecure, jeopardizing chances for a healthy development and happy childhood. In this period the way the mother is responding to emotional, physical and psychological needs of a child will condition the child's emotional base. As mentioned before, children adopt their parents' behavior, and not so rarely convictions, beliefs, emotional responses, actions, reactions and even thought patterns. Parents represent your compass, which is how a child exposed to unstable emotions, inappropriate responses and impulsive behavior noted in a borderline parent are more likely to fail in developing interpersonal functionality, while inability to regulate emotions and form meaningful relationships in adolescence and early adulthood may also appear as negative side effects of growing up with a borderline mother. Children who were brought up by a parent, or parents, suffering from borderline disorder are also more likely to develop self-harmful and destructive behavior, as well as develop increased sensitivity, vulnerability and fragility. Due to the unhealthy environment created by frequent instability and impulsive behavior expressed by borderline mothers, children may also express aggressive behavior, and develop anxiety, depressive disorders, eating disorders, PTSD, low self-esteem, and even borderline personality disorder. Older and more mature children that manage to note that something is wrong – not with them, but with their parent's behavior – may develop conditions such as depression and develop low self-esteem and issues with connecting and communicating with others due to insecurities, but are less likely to become aggressive or develop BPD themselves.

Borderline Mother: Parent-Child Relationship

Borderline mother, or a parent suffering from borderline personality disorder in general will focus on her own symptomatology rather than consider the needs obviously expressed and displayed by the child. Borderline parents often fail to see their children as individuals seeking for guidance, connection, security and recognition and are instead observed as a way of receiving self-validation as viewed from an angle of a borderline parent. Borderline mother will often take out all negative emotions on the child, using her own children as a way of venting her own insecurities, needs for affirmation and recognition, as well as annulling the fear of abandonment. In case a borderline mother is acting unnaturally calm and joyful towards the child in oppose to the usual mood swings, extreme convictions and impulsive behavior, that is usually the case because the borderline parent is fulfilling their own need for attention, recognition, love, security, validation and affection.

Moreover, borderline mother may prevent the child from expressing itself through autonomous identity, all out of fear of abandonment, while creating an atmosphere where extremes are becoming a part of everyday life. At one moment, you may feel resent and the next you may feel adored as your borderline mother is going through intense emotions and frequent mood swings. You may feel like being controlled and limited beyond comprehension where your friends are allowed to do so many things you are not allowed to, while these things are explained as "not good for you" by your mother. This is the case because a borderline mother will see your affection towards others and your connection with other people as a threat that you may abandon her. Shortly, you are finding yourself trying to fulfill every demand and request made by your borderline parent, regardless of how unstable, unrealistic and conflicted in nature these demands might be, which is usually the case when it comes to the dynamics between a borderline parent and their children. Every sign and expression of your own autonomy and identity that doesn't match your mother's demand will be controlled and limited out of fear of abandonment. The way you act, react, think and behave, which defines your identity and autonomy then soon falls under the influence of your mother's demands and expectations. She will try to prevent you from getting involved in self-exploration, as well as from expressing your own desires, inclinations, and forming your own actions and reactions. Every attempt to act as an individual is most likely to be perceived as a threat to a parent suffering from untreated borderline personality disorder.

Frequent mood changes and constant switches in emotional responses and convictions expressed by borderline mother may make you feel like everything you do is just not enough, which furthermore creates room for developing low self-esteem and insecurities, while you are more likely never to receive approval or recognition from your mother. Borderline mother is focused on the way she feels and experiences she is going through while having the need to see you and everyone else around her responding to her needs and demands – everything needs to be in line with her own emotions, mood, perception and expectations.

Children also look up to their parents in order to learn how to develop appropriate emotional responses and behavior, as well as learn how to resolve conflicts and form meaningful and complex relationships with other people. Since BPD parents are having difficulties with expressing appropriate emotional responses in addition to acting impulsively and showcasing inability to resolve conflicts with others in a healthy way, children who were brought up by BPD parents are more likely to develop some of these difficulties themselves already early in childhood, which later on becomes a more obvious problem in adulthood. As a result of growing up with borderline mother, children start to feel ashamed alongside other side-effects that come hand in hand with being brought up by a parent suffering from BPD, which may further lead to identity crisis later on in adulthood. What is perhaps the most interesting thing about parent-child dynamics in the relationship where a parent is suffering from BPD is the fact that the child will be protective in oppose to the parent despite distress and stressful childhood. You are likely to defend the parent even though your mother/father are treating you close to an object made to satisfy their need for affirmation, recognition, affection and love – all when they need it and the way they need it. You might feel like you are betraying your mother by admitting that there is a problem, which is only another side-effect of growing up with a borderline parent. Sometimes, children may even feel responsible for their parent's emotional outbursts and impulsive behavior – precisely this need to defend the parent despite obvious problems in their behavior is another way of postponing treating BPD, which is a must especially when this mental condition starts affecting children and other people around the person suffering from a borderline personality disorder. In adulthood, people who were raised by borderline mothers might even fail to recognize that the way they feel, which includes insecurities, fears, doubts, low self-esteem, guilt, depression, and disorientation of your own personality, are all actually the sub-product of growing up with a person suffering from BPD. BPD is not your fault – and it is not even your parent's fault in case the parent is able to recognize the problem and admit that something is wrong, followed with a healthy decision to start an appropriate treatment.

In order to heal from the devastating and destructive effects of being exposed to emotional and psychological instability in childhood and while growing up, you need to be ready to analyze your own psychological and emotional state and determine how you've come to feel the way you do. By successfully identifying the effects of being raised by a BPD parent, you can start healing and recovering towards relieving all the negative effects brought upon you by your borderline mother/father. In many cases, the effects of being around a BPD parent doesn't stop in adulthood, while your borderline mother may still be using you as a way of venting her own insecurities, fears and emotional instability – in this case scenario, you are most likely to put up with this behavior as you have been taught to do so through your childhood experiences. Once you decide that enough is enough, and realize that you deserve to be an individual with your own desires, inclinations and needs, you are already on the good way towards recovery. What you need to know in order to be able to do so, is that you are NOT defined by your mother's perception – the world is not defined by the way your borderline mother perceives it.

Chapter 6:

Growing Up with a Narcissistic Parent: NPD Parenting

Growing up with a narcissistic parent is rather similar to being brought up by borderline mother – the effects are devastating for child's development and may divert the child's development from a healthy path to stressful and confusing everyday life. Although there are numerous overlaps between NPD and BPD, the effects left on children growing up with NPD parent will be somewhat different than those described through growing up with borderline mother. As an adult who grew up with a narcissistic parent, often mother, you will probably be able to note that you are always striving towards perfection, but cannot explain why you feel like you can never achieve perfection at the same time. This is the case because narcissistic parents tend to criticize their children even when there is nothing wrong and despite the fact that everything is perfect or near-perfect. At last, there is no such thing as universal perfection as perfection is determined in accordance with our own standards and expectations. When it comes to expectations, narcissistic parents tend to have unrealistic expectations due to their sense of imagined perfection and superiority, However, nothing you do will ever be good enough, which is why you may doubt yourself in terms of believing that no one is right for you, as well as that you are not right for anyone. Children growing up with narcissistic parents usually try their best to impress their parents and gain recognition, affection and affirmation. Children of narcissistic parents are thus trying to earn their parent's recognition and acceptance in a way. You are likely to grow up as a happy, jumpy and cuddly child ready to learn new things and excel, which is a perfect way to raise a child, however, being raised by a narcissistic parent will make you doubt your knowledge, skills, and yourself as an individual. While your teachers will pour praises on your name, your narcissistic parent will criticize you even when it is obvious that you have done your best in something and succeeded. Your parent will miss your school plays and parent-teacher meetings, and even in case your narcissistic parent decides to attend your school play or appear at school to check your grades, you will be criticized in front of your teacher where your parent will act like you are a completely different person than you appear at school, making you look lazy, undiligent and problematic. The fact is that regardless of how hard you try to live up to expectations that a narcissist has, you will fail, not because you are unable to meet these expectations in reality, but because you won't receive any recognition due to your parent's mental condition. The worst part in this case is not that your narcissistic parent has doubts about your success in school, life and with friends, but the fact that you will be led to believe that you are indeed flawed and that there is something awfully wrong with you – this is, of course, not true, and is reflected in distorted cognition of your narcissistic parent. Just as it is the case with being raised by borderline mother, you need to understand that your parent's perception is not a realistic presentation of the world around you. So, what does it mean to be raised by a narcissist in psychosocial and emotional terms?

What Does it Mean to Be Raised by a Narcissistic Parent?

Narcissistic parents strive towards achieving perfection, however, this imagined perfection is impossible to achieve, which is how you will always try to do your best and excel in every possible field in your life, which includes friends, school and family in early days of your life. You are used to being criticized and pushed towards doing better without realizing that you are already as perfect as possible, also failing to realize that your narcissistic parent has unrealistic expectations that are impossible to fulfill the way they imagined. Even when you succeed in living up to your parent's expectations, the way you used to succeed will most likely be criticized. Children perceive their parents as guardians, guides, protectors, teachers and role models, so you will believe your mother's judgment without a question in your childhood, and even in your puberty when you are starting to look for other role models in your life. Your narcissistic parent may also try to convince you that you are selfish and not thoughtful enough, while also careless, even though you provide thoughtful tokens of attention to show your affection and gain your parent's recognition and acceptance. Your mother's lack of empathy is the thing that might affect you the most as she will not know how to come up with an appropriate emotional response when you are in distress for example, or sad, or even happy. It is most likely the case that your mother will always express the opposite of emotions you are expressing. If you are sad, she will be happy and criticize you for it, or even try to offer her help – all in favor of self-affirmation and feeding her own sense of superiority. You may even catch your mother trying to compete with you as you are growing up. Most parents have a drive to see their children doing better and becoming better people than they have become – this is less likely the case with a narcissistic parent, as narcissists will always look for ways to show their superiority and prove how they are better than other people, which includes their children as well. In your infancy stage when you are only a baby, your mother is less likely to ignore your needs and will use your existence to prove her own superiority - "Look the beautiful baby I gave birth to!". She will use you as an excuse when she is not able to achieve something in her life, so in case she had to decline a good job or leave school because she decided to give birth to you, she will make sure that you are aware of that fact and make you feel guilty about it although you didn't choose to get born – giving birth to you was your mother's choice, naturally. Your mother is less likely to be able to create meaningful relationships and friendships, so she might even try to impress your own friends, making you look dull and not as nearly as good enough as her in front of your friends. In extreme cases, a narcissist will humiliate you and emphasize your own flaws, often exaggerated and imagined, only to make you look bad. Your mother's lack of empathy and inability to find an appropriate emotional reaction when you are in distress or sad will often make you feel inappropriate, uncomfortable and like you are the one to blame for your own misfortune – instead of consoling you and making you feel better, she will only make things worse by criticizing you and making you take the blame for the way you feel. This case scenario may make you retreat to yourself and stop sharing your thoughts and emotions, not only with your mother, but with other people who might understand what you are going through. A child of a narcissist is less likely to become a narcissist itself in adult life, although there are cases where a narcissist has been brought up by a person suffering from a narcissistic personality disorder. This relation may appear as "clash of titans" with ever-present conflicts between two personalities with stubborn conviction of entitlement and superiority. Just as in the case with being raised by a BPD parent, narcissist will reflect their fears on their children, also displaying fear of being abandoned and fear of never achieving perfection. This is how you may grow up to live with insecurities and relationship issues. Even in case your mother actually feels love for you, narcissistic personality disorder will make her unable to show that affection in an appropriate way, so you may never feel truly loved. What is interesting is that children usually don't blame the mother for this case, believing that they are somehow responsible for the lack of affection and empathy, so naturally, these children will try to meet the mother's needs at all times. Narcissistic parent also tends to separate children, so in case you have siblings, you will notice that your mother is favorizing one of you. Even if you are her "favorite" child, you will come to realize after a while that your mother is complaining on you to your siblings, and even friends, while she will likewise complain about your siblings to you. Her need to criticize will be stronger than the lowest level of devotion she might have for her children. In case you fail to meet any of her unrealistic demands, you will probably be exposed to impulsive and dangerous behavior, while you will be forced to take blame for everything she finds "wrong" or disturbing. The most important thing you need to note when being raised by a narcissist and later on in your adult life, that you should never hold demands of a narcissistic parent logical or realistic. In conclusion, you shouldn't allow yourself to be defined by your mother's perception as you will never be able to find peace in yourself.

Growing Up with a Narcissist: Parent-Child Dynamics

You might recognize some of the following behavior patterns in case you were raised by a narcissistic mother. Starting off with early childhood, the effects of living with a narcissistic parent will already become obvious during the verbal stage of a child. Children are happy with slightest achievements they make, like learning how to tie shoelaces or draw their first smiley face, and naturally, parents should react with encouragement and praise. Narcissistic mothers will either be unwilling or unable to recognize their children's effort, which is why it is likely that they will fail in praising their children. Instead, they are less likely to criticize a child as if it was a grown-up with fully developed skills and personality. This behavior is enticed by the sense of superiority and imagined perfection. Let's say that a child expresses a desire to play football, naturally, the child might ask to join a local team that trains juniors and encourages children that are able to express talent in the game. Narcissistic mother is less likely to allow the child to go for football despite openly expressed interest, and will discourage the child from joining the team – this behavior may be expressed both through claims of affection "I love you and I know what's best for you" and criticism "You don't have an idea on how football is played. Football is not for you". This is only a trivial example of how narcissistic parent will try, and in many cases succeed in having their way. Growing up with narcissistic parent, you will feel oppressed and suffocated at times and frequently, as anything that makes you happy will find criticism from your parent's side. What is also symptomatic behavior expressed by narcissists is the fact that your mother will be there for you when you are not doing that well – this is not because you are loved with no conditions, but because narcissistic parents thrive in their children's misery. As you are growing up, you will notice that your mother is always there when you are having issues in school, with your friends, girlfriends or boyfriends, or problems with finances and work, while you are constantly criticized when you are obviously doing great. The most common side-effect of growing up with a narcissistic mother is developing insecurities and low self-esteem, which appears as a result of frequent criticism directed towards you and your individuality. You will catch yourself doing anything to make your parent happy, but nothing you do will be good enough. Narcissistic parent might even try convincing you into believing that you are no good for anyone, emphasizing her love for you despite all the flaws she can see in your character. These "flaws" are usually expressions of your own individuality which is getting in the way of the need of your parent to control you and your perception of the world around you. Your parent may even take credit for everything you do well in cases where criticism doesn't feel like an option, as narcissists believe that they deserve recognition for things they didn't achieve. Narcissists also enjoy to be in the center of attention, which means that you have probably suffered a great deal in your adolescence once your interest was directed towards spending more time with your friends, which is a perfectly normal thing as you are developing your psychosocial skills. To make you switch your attention back to your narcissistic parent, which is often the case with mothers who are suffering from NPD, your mother will criticize your friends, or act acceptive towards your friends and criticize you in front of them with the goal of making them leave you so she could have you all for herself. She always "knows the best" and she likes to use "I told you so" whenever something bad happens to you "...but you didn't listen to your mother."

In order to remain in the center of attention, your mother will prevent you from going out and meeting your friends and will use the most illogical excuses to explain why you need to stay home or get back earlier than your friends. She will not stand any attempt of having you convince her that she is wrong – her sense of supremacy and entitlement is making her believe that her perception is correct and that she is only right. The most devastating effect that growing up with NPD parent may leave on you is disabling you from developing your own identity – any attempt of secrecy and individuality will be stopped by NPD parent as narcissistic parent wants to know everything you do, think, feel or believe without actually acknowledging your perception and cognition. You may also notice that your parent is envious and jealous of your success later in your adult life, which is when you might notice that you are going through an abusive cycle that will never stop until you are ready to get out of that vicious circle. The fact is that you will never get an honest recognition for your achievements, while you will be criticized for every single thing you believe you have done well. Later on when you become a parent yourself, your mother/father will undermine you in front of your own children and criticize your parenting – it is a never-ending circle in which you are set to suffer unless you decide to act in accordance with your individuality and not in line with unrealistic and false expectations of your narcissistic parent.

After we have defined borderline personality disorder and narcissistic personality disorder, and presented how it appears to be growing up and being raised by BPD and NPD parents, it is time to help you recover from any potential and negative side effects that BPD and NPD parenting might have left on you. In the following chapter, you will find numerous and helpful techniques and tips on how to recover from being brought up by NPD and BPD parent.

Chapter 7:

How to Recover from Toxic Parenting and Overcome Childhood Trauma

Unfortunately, you probably decided not to tell anyone about what you were going through while living with a parent, or parents, with unstable emotions, impulsive behavior and questionable parenting methods that all appear as a result of having a parent suffering from narcissistic personality disorder and borderline personality disorder, which is why you were probably struggling with finding ways to survive your childhood in case you were aware of the effects your parent's NPD or BPD is leaving on you. In many cases, children who were raised and brought up by parents or a parent suffering from untreated NPD and BPD developed BPD themselves, depression, anxiety, fears, antisocial behavior, self-doubts, low self-esteem, problems with relationships, distorted image of personal identity, identity crisis, insecurities, eating disorders and even PTSD. The first step towards recovering from devastating and damaging effects of being raised by borderline parents or narcissistic parents is to realize that you have your own identity that needs to be nurtured and developed in a way that wasn't possible during your childhood. To start your journey towards recovery and annulation of these damaging effects, you need to realize that something is wrong in the way you were brought up, which you already did as you are reading this guide. We will try to guide you to your recovery by presenting numerous techniques and treatments that can help you rebuild your identity and rise above being raised by borderline mother or narcissistic parent.

#1 Realization: It Is Not Your Fault

The first step towards your recovery is to let you know something that should have been told to you long ago: It is not your fault. It is not your fault that you have had the misfortune to be raised by a parent suffering from NPD or BPD. You probably already feel uncomfortable for even reading direct criticism describing your NPD/BPD parent as you might have learned to observe things through the lens of distorted cognition served up by your parent. There were probably tones of times when you felt guilty or ashamed for even thinking that something is wrong with your parent, as parents should be the first role models a child looks up to, as well as represent your first relationship model. Parents should teach you how to resolve conflicts and how to develop appropriate reactions in accordance with experiences and situations you encounter, but since their cognition is distorted due to NPD or BPD, it is difficult for a child to comprehend that there is something wrong. Children are looking up to their parents and are counting on their support, love, devotion, help, guidance, affection and recognition, which is why children may not realize that their parents are doing something which goes against the child's advantage. There might be some divided opinions on whether you should blame a parent who is suffering from a mental disorder in case they are not aware of their own condition, however, some parents may refuse to get a treatment even when they are aware of their symptomatic behavior. The person who decides to point out that problem is more likely to be accused to be envious, jealous, a liar, and is perceived as someone who means harm, which may further go to demonization even though that person's perception is on point. Regardless of the past that you need to make peace with and overcome your traumatic experiences from childhood, your journey must start with realization that the way you were treated by your parent is not in any way your fault, and can never be your fault.

#2 Regression: Getting Back to Past Experiences

Although it might be difficult for you to go back to some experiences you had as a child and while growing up with BPD or NPD parent, you need to go back and trace everything you suspect your mother did wrong in her parenting. You may feel fear as you start to criticize your mother in your thoughts, which is only the cause of effects your mother's condition left on you in the past while you were growing up – all human beings make mistakes and errors, and the mere fact that a narcissist or a person suffering from borderline personality disorder is not able to set right from wrong, and take responsibility for their actions, confirms that parents also make mistakes. Unfortunately, these mistakes may leave a strong imprint on the child, like it might be in your own case. By analyzing your parent's behavior and getting back to your childhood experiences, you can think through every situation in your family that made you feel uncomfortable. If NPD or BPD parent was to face you within your experience, you would probably be told that you are ungrateful and probably convinced that anything bad that had happened was actually your fault, directly or indirectly. However, you no longer want to be defined by your parent's identity so you are set to roam free through your experiences and memories. As you are remembering, you need to try not to seek for justifications for your parent's behavior in the past, and in the present in case you are still falling under the influence of your parent's mental state. By going back to your past experiences, you will be able to question things that made you feel lost, unloved, confused, ashamed and triggered doubts and other negative emotions and thoughts and ask yourself if what you feel was defined by you or by someone else, in this case by your parent. The main goal in this practice is to reveal the truth about the relationship you have with your parent, identify your parent's identity and separate it from yours.

#3 Individuality: The Importance of Individual Identity

Identity is defined by your sense of self and a set of values you have adopted while growing up. As you are developing as a person, your identity is developing alongside, while prone to change, as well as the effects of internal and external factors. The sense of self appears already in the early age and during childhood as you are slowly starting to realize that you are an individual with your own needs, inclinations, characteristics and desires. Value is usually "inherited" from parents as children look up to their parents as the first role models they have in life, which is why growing up in a healthy family is essential for child's development. NPD and BPD parents have distorted cognition as one of the main symptoms triggered by these mental conditions, which is how their set of values is set to be distorted likewise. The child can't be aware of the fact that the values taught to him are actually wrong in oppose to what is normal in general, however, despite the lack of awareness and child's innocence and trust in his parents, adopting a false or negative set of values will affect the child during childhood and further in adolescence towards adulthood. One of the heaviest side effects that growing up with NPD and BPD parents leaves on you is the lack of individuality and value of your own identity. NPD and BPD parents and their behavior patterns are preventing the child from developing a healthy sense of self, while any attempt of the child to act as an individual is usually prevented and criticized with the goal of keeping the child close to the family. Every healthy and happy person is certain in their own sense of self and is aware of their own identity, and while a healthy and happy person can understand diversity of other people's identities, they are still set to develop and nurture their own individuality. It is precisely that individuality that you might have been robbed for during your childhood. Strong identity and sense of self allows people to refuse something without feeling bad for saying NO, it enables healthy relationships with other people, allows you to give and share without feeling used or being used, and enables you to ask for what you deserve. Children who grew up with narcissistic or borderline parents, usually don't have the courage to accept any of the qualities listed above due to the weak sense of self and the lack of personal identity.

#4 Your Parent Has a Choice, You Have a Choice

Many people will argue that NPD and BPD, especially BPD, are serious mental conditions and should be treated, observed and understood as such, stressing out that people who are suffering from narcissistic or borderline disorder shouldn't be blamed for their condition. These conditions come with negative and dangerous behavior patterns, as well as actions and reactions that could bring damage to people around patients with NPD and BPD. Based on the mentioned opinion, people suffering from BPD and NPD then shouldn't take responsibility for their actions. However, someone has to. This burden is usually fully disclosed to children growing up with NPD and BPD parents, who are taking blame, negative effects, and responsibility for their parent's actions. As a child, you may not be aware that something is wrong with your parent and the way you are being raised, but as you are developing and socializing, meeting friends and their own families, you will certainly notice that the way you are being raised is somewhat different when compared to the way your friends are being treated by their parents. This is the time when you might realize that your parent has a serious problem and that this problem is affecting you. As a child, you might be too scared to react or even feel ashamed for thinking that there is something wrong with your parents, however, you have a choice to come out clean and state what you want to say. Once your parent is faced to a possibility that something is seriously wrong in the way they act, react and behave, they have a choice as well. Unfortunately, since BPD and NPD patients have distorted cognition and false sense of reality, they are less likely to consider that there is a problem in the way they behave – this would be specifically difficult for people suffering from NPD, as they have an increased sense of self-importance, entitlement and superiority. Regardless of your age and your parent's age, you still have a choice to speak up and state your mind about the way you feel affected by your parent's condition. In order to do so, you don't even have to directly confront your NPD/BPD parent – instead, you can make peace with yourself and make it your choice to break the cycle of fulfilling your parents unrealistic expectations.

#5 Expression: Work on Your Individuality

To loosen the effects of growing up with a narcissist or a parent suffering from BPD, you need to start expressing yourself and find your own individuality. There is no magic formula that could help you achieve that, but the solution for the problem is rather simple – you just need to analyze yourself, in terms of exploring your needs, goals, objectives and desires. You are not due to obey your parent's vision of the world and their perception of your own experiences. Even if you make a wrong choice, that is perfectly all right, because you are making a choice that you can call YOUR own. There is no right or wrong in this case – the perception of the black-and-white world is actually facilitated by your parent who is unable to see that there is a middle – the grey area – between the black-and-white and right and wrong. Start with simple things like playing music you really like and turning the volume up to sooth your own mood. Explore your own desires and objectives and set goals for yourself that you will gladly work on in order to achieve what you want. Choose your own friends, your own profession, your own job, because you were not born to live someone else's life even if it is your parent's life that has been imposed on you. In cases where there are siblings and a child growing up with NPD and BPD parent is not the only child in the family, one child – usually the eldest – becomes an object of parentification. Parentification signifies the case where a parent, usually suffering from NPD, is teaching one of the children to become a "foster parent" by taking care of the household, parents and other children in the family. That way, the child loses its individuality in a way, while a great number of tasks and commitments may get in the way of individual and personal success. Because of this case, you can develop an increased sense of empathy and the need to help others even when you are neglecting your own personal necessities and commitments, and developing the feeling that you need to serve and help. This is another way how children growing up with NPD and BPD parents can lose a sense of self as well as their individuality. Don't miss on asking yourself "What do I need?", "What do I want?", "Is this something I want?" – try to be as honest as possible and don't panic if you feel like you should say NO to some things that get in the way of your happiness and comfort. For once, you should focus on building your own self and rebuilding what has been "damaged" by the devastating influence of your parent. Express yourself!

#6 Get Rid of the Guilt

As a child that grew up with either NPD or BPD parent, you have most likely developed a sense of constant or frequent guilt. This is the case because you encountered blame from your parent's side every time you asked for something, expressed your needs, or when you were unable to meet your parent's expectations. Moreover, NPD and BPD parents tend to blame their children for distress they feel personally as caused by their mental condition, which is why you may feel guilty even for things that don't have anything to do with you. For example, let's say that you are meeting your friend at a café. Your friend looks particularly agitated and irritated although he or she is trying her best to be in the good mood. Your friend is not disclosing the reason for the way they feel, so you naturally presume that you have caused that negative feeling even though you are certain that you did nothing wrong. Instead of asking your friend if everything is alright, you are likely to jump to conclusions and come up with attaching responsibility for your friend's bad mood to yourself, which leads to feeling guilty. In order to overcome this problem, you need to practice preventing yourself from jumping to conclusions that would confirm the fear of perpetual guilt. You can fight your feeling of guilt with facts, truth and communication with your friend in this case. Instead of jumping to a conclusion that your friend is in a bad mood because of you, you can just ask "Is everything all right? You look like you are having a bad time". Your friend will surely tell you what the problem is about, which will consequently lead to realization that you are not responsible for the way your friend feels. You can practice this simple technique every time you are in doubt and you think that you did something wrong due to which you are feeling guilty. You can also ask yourself: "Is there REALLY something I did to make this happen?" - in this case that would be the bad mood your friend is experiencing. The answer to this question should be based solely on facts and truth, while you will as well avoid jumping to conclusions. Automated guilt and frequently blaming yourself for things that are happening around you is just a side effect that appears as a result for being blamed by your parent and being forced to take responsibility even when you were not responsible in any way. Some people who were raised by NPD and BPD parents, especially those growing up with narcissists, will also have a feeling of guilt for things that are happening to them and which cannot be controlled. For example, let's say that you lose your job because there were technical cuts in the company you worked for. Technically, it is not your fault that you got fired because you did nothing wrong to cause the distress of losing your job – becoming a part of technical cuts is the case scenario that is most obviously out of your control, which means that there is nothing you could have done to assure keeping your job. However, somehow you end up blaming yourself and thinking that there is probably something you could have done to prevent this misfortunate event. Accepting the fact that sometimes bad things happen with no reason or sense is the first step towards preventing yourself from taking blame and feeling guilty.

#7 Learn How to Say NO When You Need To

As a child of NPD or BPD parent it is most likely the case that you have never learned how to say NO to things you don't feel like doing and other people's requests. You are used to completing unrealistic demands and requests imposed by your parent, so this is something you started to feel comfortable with although you may feel like being in distress deep within. You wanted to gain your parent's recognition, attention and affection, so you always tried your best to do exactly as told without questioning your parents unrealistic expectations and motives. Later on, you are noticing your own inability to say NO to other people, so you wind up fulfilling other people's needs and demands all out of need to please and help others. Your inability to say NO when it feels right to refuse something might feel debilitating and is certainly preventing you from expressing yourself. One of the ways to express your individuality is to decide what feels right and what doesn't. It is perfectly fine to say NO when you feel like saying NO – otherwise, you will continue to place other people's needs before your own. You can't please others on the expense of your own happiness and comfort, and as soon as you learn how to say NO when you feel like it is the right thing to do, the sooner you will be able to regain your own self that has been taken from you while you were growing up. Let's say that your mother with NPD is insisting that you should come to here and help her with something she considers to be very important, although the importance of this matter is questionable to you. At the same time, you have arranged your own plans that somehow match your mother's plans. What will you do? Say: "Yes, I'll be there right away" without even mentioning that you have already made plans of your own? In case you are still stuck in the vicious cycle you have become a part of since your childhood, you will say YES without even mentioning your own needs and placing your mother's needs ahead of yours. However, if you are slowly starting to feel like the effects of your childhood are fading due to your will to get better and feel better, you will say: "Sorry mom, I already have something else planned, but I can help you with that some other time if you'd like." You are more likely to get a ton of criticism from the other side as your parent is probably used to having you available for any kind of demand and request they might have for you. In this case you should remember that you are your own person with the right to choose how you spend your time. When you think about it, time equals life as our life on earth is inevitably limited by our nature, so ask yourself if you are ready to spend your time on living other people's lives instead living your own life.

#8 Improving Your Sense of Self

In order to improve your sense of self, you need to give yourself what you have been giving others. That means that you need to empathize with yourself and accept yourself for who you are. You shouldn't be running from your past – you should utilize your past experiences in order to determine what to do and what to avoid doing. By being aware of all the positive and negative things in your life, you can work on enhancing positivity and reducing negative influences of your past. Make peace with your childhood and the way you were raised, as well as experiences you went through to learn a valuable lesson – one of the lessons you need to learn in order to set yourself free is that you may hardly live a happy life if you don't have yourself. You may start with improving yourself by practicing tracing your own emotions and analyzing why you feel the way you feel. Any emotion that you are experiencing based on your negative thoughts or getting back to past should be thoroughly analyzed and made peace with. For example, you are lying down on your bed and your hands are set on your belly. You are breathing in and out, slowly following your breathing tempo. How do you feel? Did something good happen today at work and you still feel like there is something wrong? You feel that you are not good enough and that the good thing that happened is not enough to make you feel better about yourself? Ask yourself why is this the case. If you don't have a logical answer that could be proven with facts and if your negative emotions are related to your parent, you should imagine that feeling fading away. You can imagine swimming in the ocean while all negativity is being washed away until you are able to experience the good thing that happened to you. Be grateful and happy for discovering a positive emotion and managing to wipe the bad things away. Focus on how you feel, versus how your past experiences are conditioning you to feel. You need to realize that some negative emotions that you are feeling and that are not backed by actual events that are taking place in the present, actually represent leftovers from your parent's influence and should be switched for more positive experiences and emotions that belong to you. Even when you are faced with negative experiences in the present, you should accept these experiences and triggered emotions as a part of your own self. Beside from tracing your emotions, you can improve your sense of self by listing your own flaws and traits then analyzing the list in order to determine which traits and flaws are actually and realistically yours and which were prescribed to you by your mother without any logic.

#9 Improving Your Social Interactions

Growing up with NPD and BPD parent can rob you of proper way of interacting socially as you may find yourself retreating from any form of social interactions because you feel like you don't have anything interesting or clever to say, or because you believe that you are just not good enough for other people. The feeling that other people might not be good enough for you and that there are many ways in which you can be betrayed and let down may also appear as a consequence from being raised by NPD or BPD parent. Narcissistic parents tend to convince their children that there is no one in the world that could love them as they do, which is the consequence of their fear of abandonment and anxiety that they will seize to be in the center of attention. They will prevent you from growing up as an individual, which includes making friends and getting involved in social interactions. When your parent wouldn't be able to prevent you from making friends, they are likely to come up with ridiculous and unrealistic excuses on why you can't go out with your friends, or why you need to be home early when all your friends are staying.

All these actions may cause you to retreat to social isolation and stop making efforts in making friends and meeting new people. Your BPD or NPD parent may also try to convince you that everyone you know is actually making fun of you and that they are your friends because they want or need something from you and not because you are an interesting person to be around. This case may cause you to doubt anyone and everyone is intention, making you develop mistrustful behavior in combination with isolation. To break this cycle, you need to allow others to get close to you and open yourself to meeting new people, going out and develop meaningful relationships with people. You need to be aware that as someone who has spent a great part of their life with NPD or BPD parent, you may have developed a tendency to seek connection with people who are emotionally demanding and dominant as you need to express the taught need to please others and fulfill unrealistic demands – avoid getting into this type of relationships so you would avoid maintaining a toxic relationship. Fear of being rejected and not being accepted is possibly present as well, but you must fight this feeling and go against your fear in order to be able to communicate with other people and improve your social life.

#10 Learn How to Deal with Conflicts

NPD and BPD parents are not able to resolve conflicts in an appropriate way and by talking things through. When you were living with your parent, you have surely gotten into a conflict more than once without even realizing why something you did represented a problem, while you were often drawn into conflicts without any logical reason whatsoever. Conflict resolution probably consisted of shouting, pointing fingers, back turning and leaving the room, pouring accusations and involved illogical arguments. There were no boundaries, no compromises and no valid arguments, while your parent most likely never came to an agreement in any of these arguments. This may have affected you in a way that you would always choose to make a compromise as long as that would mean that the conflict is resolved, while your boundaries may be undefined and unlimited. This case would make you lose your self-respect along the way, also making you unable to resolve conflicts in a healthy manner. Learning how to appropriately resolve conflicts is very important because conflicts are natural part of any type of relationship and happen from time to time. Being frequently conflicted with someone is not healthy and rather represents a sign of having an unhealthy relationship with someone. To make sure that you are able to resolve your conflicts in a healthy way, there are some things that you need to learn:

- **Boundaries** – You need to set some boundaries in advance, so you would know when is the right time to retreat and stop the argument leading to nowhere. If the person you are having an argument with starts with insults, swearing and shouting, your boundaries are crossed and broken and you may retreat as it is obvious that no conflict can be resolved by creating more conflicts. Setting boundaries means having self-respect. You should likewise respect the boundaries of the opposite party and avoid creating more conflict when unnecessary. Respect has to be mutual at all times.

- *Tracing Issues* – You need to go through all issues that caused the conflict in the first place – you may only use facts and truth in order to determine what's wrong and find an appropriate solution. Logic and calmness are your best friends here.

- *Compromising* – Agreeing to a compromise is a great part of the overall conflict resolution and sometimes may be the only way to resolve an active conflict. You and the other party may agree to "meet each other halfway", that way coming to a resolution that would be partially convenient for both sides.

- *Arguments* – Arguments have to be truthful, logical and based on facts, otherwise, the conflict may only become worse. Try to leave emotions aside when listing arguments as conflicts usually give

birth to explosive emotions that may lead
to impulsive behavior.

- ***Agree to Disagree*** – You may also
  agree to disagree and leave the argument
  as it is while at the same time resolving a
  conflict. Make sure that you and the other
  party both agree to disagree, otherwise
  the problem may reappear.

#11 Resolving Chronic Self-blame

You have probably taken a good portion of blame
while you were growing up as NPD and BPD
parents tend to find guilt in people that actually
don't have anything to do with their initial
problem in the first place. You are most likely to
be one of those people, i.e. victims of distorted
reality and increased self-importance. Believing
in your parent's judgment, you've been silently
dealing with taking blame to the point where you
are slowly starting to adopt a chronic self-blame.
Whenever something bad happens, although you
had nothing to do with it, you feel like you are the
one to blame. The way other people feel, act and
behave, experiences and events that cannot be
controlled by your abilities or will – you
somehow manage to blame it all on yourself. The
best way of getting rid of self-blame is to start
actualizing the way you are blaming yourself for
different things and events. Whenever you feel

guilty and start blaming yourself, stop and consider the facts. What do the facts state? How did you end up being responsible for something that happened? Are you personally and directly responsible for the negative event you are blaming yourself for? The answer probably includes the key to resolving your case of self-blame. Facts and logic will become your best friends in this case.

#12 Find Your Own Voice: Anti-echoism

If we turn back to mythology, we can remember the story of Narcissus – a beautiful man that fell in love with his own image as well as the story about Echo – a beautiful nymph that fell in love with beautiful, but self-centered and proud Narcissus. Echo was doomed to repeat only the words spoken by others, which is why her love remained unfulfilled among other factors and Narcissus' inability to love anything or anyone except feel attracted to his own image. Echoism, based on the Greek mythology about poor Echo, actually represents one of the side-effects from being raised by a narcissistic parent. Echoism involves repeating thoughts, statements, convictions, and behaviors imposed by NPD parent while making you unable to come up with your own words, reactions and actions that match your character and identity. Later in your adult life you may even express echoism with other people and easily adopt their own perception of reality, which is actually a toxic behavior preventing you from reaffirming your own personal identity. As an echoes, you are more likely to be truly happy about other people's achievements while having little or no regard for your own achievements and considering that nothing you do is actually worth mentioning. You are ready to help anyone and everyone, but will never ask for help yourself; you are honestly complimenting others, while you have a difficult time accepting compliments yourself. There is no way of getting rid of echoism if you are not aware of this trait – you need to work on your self-esteem and developing the sense of self in order to be able to accept yourself as someone is actually worth. Every time you achieve a goal, treat yourself, praise yourself and be happy about your success as much as you are happy with other people's success. This may be difficult to do at first, but by practicing praising yourself for your own achievements as often as possible and accepting your self-worth will work benevolently on diminishing devastating effects of echoism.

#13 Insecurity and Attachment

The inability of your parent to praise you and recognize your achievements in a perpetual way has probably made you insecure of who you are and your own skills, talents and abilities as nothing is good enough for your parent. On the other hand, you have probably spent your childhood listening to your parent convincing you into believing that no one will ever love you the way they do. In combination with unhealthy attachment your parent, usually mother, imposed on you, you have probably developed a great number of insecurities regarding yourself and others, which might be getting in the way of forming, developing and maintaining relationships with others. You may be fearful that you will get abandoned, hurt and let down, or your insecurities of attachment may drive you to become too obsessed with everything that could go wrong in case you open yourself to others. You may also feel like you don't need anyone to be happy and that you are fine on your own, but secretly you feel lonely. Even if you manage to form a relationship with someone in case you feel you don't need anyone, you may treat that person as if they were just passing by through your life with no means to keep them close, which eventually drives them away from you. So, investing yourself too much in a relationship or not being invested enough may both represent issues for the way you are developing and maintaining relationships. If you don't get over your insecurities and attachment issues, you may end up alone and away from people you really care about, while change starts with changing your own perspective of intimacy and relationships. For starters, you should try and form connections with people who have secure attachment as you could use a healthier perspective and silent guidance on how intimacy and healthy attachment should look like. Another helpful thing to do to get closer to resolving your insecurities and attachment issues is to follow your attachment patterns and behavior and stop them at core as soon as you notice that something is wrong and that you are not acting appropriately. Neediness, insecurities and fear of being abandoned may all be resolved rather simply if you make an extra mile in observing and tracing your own behavior and switching it to more productive and positive patterns. You should first realize that it all starts from your traumatic childhood and thought patterns you have adopted during that stage of your life. The very realization that you have been taught against your will how to develop insecurities and attachment issues, may help you reaffirm your identity and change these toxic patterns. One of the most important things to do when recovering is to develop awareness of patterns that are negative and try to replace them with more constructive behavior.

#14 Regaining Trust in People

Displaying trust issues and having a difficult time trusting other people is another problem that appears with growing up with NPD or BPD parents. The effects of growing up with borderline mother or narcissistic parent may make you feel like you can't trust anyone and that everyone will let you down in case you let your guard down. To start the process of regaining trust in others, you first need to start trusting yourself, and by that we mean that you need to trust your own feelings – not thought patterns and behaviors you were taught to believe by your parent. Trust your gut, trust your emotions and trust yourself when you feel like you can actually connect with someone and trust someone. Rebuilding trust is not an easy task, as you need to motivate yourself into doing so – in a way, you need to make a leap of trust and just let go off your fears and the idea that you can trust no one. Sounds easier than it actually is? Of course, it does. But that doesn't mean that regaining trust in people is impossible. You might have had bad experiences with unsuccessful and consuming relationships where you have been betrayed and let down, led to believe that your parent was right all along in their conviction that you can really trust no one. However, you shouldn't allow yourself to give up on the first sign of failure as not all people are the same and you need to know that you deserve someone who also deserves your trust. You need to be willing to take a risk and trusting someone, so even if a mistake is made, you can learn how to spot signs in a person that can't be trusted. You should, however, never apply the same pattern you have noted on all people you try to make a connection with. You also need to learn that trust needs to be earned from both sides and that this process has its own natural course that takes time. Start from basics – allow someone you want to make a connection with to enter your life then try to build your way up to trust that person and allow them to show you that they could be trusted. Mistakes will certainly be made, but that is only a part of life itself as no one is perfect regardless of false perception your NPD parent might have imposed on you. You should also note that not all mistakes that are made in a relationship represent broken trust – making mistakes is a normal part of any and every relationship which can be resolved by talking and agreeing to a compromise in case the mistake is justified.

#15 Recognize and Acknowledge Your Needs

You are probably used to recognizing other people's needs rather well, while taking little or no regard for your own needs and wants. You are used to fulfilling your parents unrealistic expectations and being there whenever you were needed, which is why you have no or little skills in recognizing and acknowledging your own needs and necessities. You need to decide that it is finally the time for you to start taking care for yourself. Caring for others is a beautiful trait to have, but allowing yourself to give your last breath to others on the cost of your own wellbeing and happiness is a flaw you can't afford in the process of healing from the effects of being raised by NPD and BPD parents. Another step towards developing your sense of self and working on improving the image you have of yourself, as well as developing your own identity is realizing that you have needs that seek for acknowledgment and recognition. Ask yourself, what do you need today? Try starting from simple needs like going out for your favorite meal with a good friend, then take it from there to more complex needs such as your relationship goals, professional goals and emotional needs. In the process, try to separate things you think you need and that appear as a side effect from your childhood trauma, and needs that you actually know are a part of yourself.

#16 Care for Your Own Happiness

Life is a combination of good times and bad times in a nutshell, so it is perfectly normal to be down at times, while a couple of "bad" days are usually annulled by a week of good days. In case you are noticing that you are inclined towards perpetual sadness and that it is very difficult to be happy for more than a day even when you have lots of reasons to be happy, that probably means that you are not used to just relaxing and caring for your own happiness. The chances are that you are so used to making other people happy that you stopped considering that you should make yourself happy as well. Embrace happy days whenever you are faced to a positive experience or event – savor it and enjoy it with your lungs full. Work towards your own happiness as you would work on making someone else happy, all while accepting the fact that you deserve to be happy.

#17 Life is Not a Threat

Due to the way you have been treated in your childhood, you might have developed a feeling of constant survival, which makes you unable to relax and observe some things as trivial. You may also develop a sense of doom that makes you feel like everything will turn out in the most horrible way so you must be on the constant lookout to prevent bad case scenarios from happening – all these false convictions and emotions are making you perceive life as a threat. The world is NOT going to collapse on your shoulders if you decide to take a break and relax. You have to know that not everything will fall apart if you relax and take a nap. You may even have difficulties with your sleeping patterns with a perpetual feeling of extramural experiences and events. Yes, life can be difficult as your own childhood has proven to you, however, life can be likewise beautiful and somewhat careless at times – you just need to decide what you want your life to become. By adopting more positive thought patterns, you will be able to come to a stage where you no longer feel like you are in survival mode all the time. The constant pressure that you have been experiencing through your childhood and adolescence have probably made you get used to constantly being under stress as there are numerous expectations that you need to live up to. Set your own set of rules and expectations and try to remove stress as an ever-present factor. Life is more than surviving – always remember that you deserve more than just surviving: pep-talk yourself into believing in value of life if you need to.

#18 Your Trauma Doesn't Define You

The fact that you went through a series of misfortunate experiences, effects and events does not define who you are in reality – it rather defines a version of you that was created by your parent who taught you into believing that they know what is best for you, when in reality their behavior only brought you insecurities and issues that you need to resolve on your own. Your traumatic events define you only in case you allow that. By giving into your past traumatic experiences, you are actually strengthening your issues, fears and insecurities, which is why you need to realize that you are not what your parent taught you to be – you are your own person and no one can take that from you unless you allow it. You have the freedom to allow or not allow your traumas to define who you are and who you wish to become. Traumatic experiences in reality only define a part of your life – your traumatic past, which should be resolved in order to invite happiness into your life.

#19 Living Up to Your Own Expectations

By far, you have been living up to other people's expectations, which includes your NPD or BPD parents who often find the most unrealistic expectations and expect you to be there for every request, need and requirement, regardless of how absurd it may sound to you – and the worst thing is that you were always there to give your best regardless of the fact that you are not even receiving any recognition from others. For a change, you should set your own expectations, and list them as your goals, while being aware that these goals and expectations are set to become achievements that will make you proud of who you've become. Don't think about what your parents or other people will say – setting your own expectations is purely your own concern. Instead of trying to fulfill ridiculous and unrealistic goals and expectations set by your parent or other people, you should focus on what you wish to achieve in life, looking up to your own expectations without including other people in this equation. Do you really believe that you were born to maker other people happy on the cost of your own happiness? Hopefully, the answer is NO.

#20 Be Proud of Yourself and Your Achievements

As someone who was raised by BPD and NPD parent, you are probably having issues with recognizing your own achievements, which is most likely the case because you have never gotten any form of recognition from your parent regardless of how well you do. It can be the case that you've grown tired of living up to your parent's expectations, so you became an underachiever, uninterested in your own development and success. This has to change in order to find your own self. Set your goals straight and work on achieving them. There is no magic formula for this, yet again, while you need to motivate yourself into recognizing your achievements, to the point where you can say that you are proud of yourself. This probably wouldn't be easy as you have rarely heard that someone is proud of you, especially your parent, however, by recognizing that you have made a positive change that made an impact on your life, you are already taking the first step towards becoming proud of your own achievements. In the beginning, it may feel like you are forcing yourself to develop a sense of pride towards your own positive actions, which is not far from the truth. However, by encouraging yourself to provide positive affirmations for your own achieved goals, you are getting closer to learning how to appreciate yourself.

#21 Anxiety and Depression

Many children who were raised by NPD and BPD parents end up developing anxiety disorders and depressive disorders later in adolescence and adulthood. Neglect, criticism, lack of attention and recognition, expectations and exposure to living with a parent who is suffering from mental disorder, is all taking its toll on you, which may result in developing anxiety and depression despite the fact that you were probably a joyful and cuddly child during your childhood. Depression may come in many forms and appear systematically, periodically or triggered by an event or experience that resembles your past traumatic experiences, while the same goes for developing anxiety disorder. Constant distress, stressful childhood, lack of appreciation and affection from your parent may all push you towards damaging and dangerous behavior while some people tend to turn to alcohol and drug abuse believing they would get better thanks to the chemical escapism they are involved in. Anxiety and depression usually start from developing negative thought patterns with negative inner dialogues and conclusions that show detachment from reality. Furthermore, depression and anxiety may lead to suicidal thoughts and dangerous behavior that leads to self-harm. That is how it is of crucial importance to treat your condition if you notice that you are displaying symptoms of anxiety and/or depression. Lack of motivation, perpetual sadness, fears and phobias, frequent feeling of despair and doom, and inability to embrace happiness and enjoy in things you once found pleasurable are all symptoms that may indicate that you are suffering from depression or anxiety. In case you feel like you are not able to resolve your mental condition by yourself and by adopting more positive thoughts and behavior patterns that will pull you out of despair, you should try and look for help and talk to a therapist. Avoid getting depression medications if that is possible and try out talk therapies such as cognitive behavioral therapy, based on changing thoughts in order to change emotions and behavior.

#22 Truth and Facts Against Imagined Reality and Distorted Cognition

People suffering from narcissistic personality disorder and bipolar personality disorder rely on their own cognition and perception, which is actually distorted – that means that the way they perceive reality and the world around them is not based on FACTS. Their perception is instead based on the way they feel about reality, which doesn't depict the true image of the world, experiences and events taking place around them. Parents suffering from NPD and BPD tend to impose their perception on their children, while the child belies them unconditionally and tends to accept their parent's version of reality. Later in adolescence and adulthood, this distorted perception comes to an emphasis, so you may end up dealing with distorted cognition with absence of facts even though your perception is different than the one your parents imposed on you. So instead of thinking that you are the most perfect creature in the world without the ability to make mistakes, which is the case with NPD parents and represent distorted cognition, you may end up believing that you are not good enough regardless of what you are able to achieve. You may end up believing that everyone will let you down and that there is no one who can love you the way you are able to give love to others. You may end up believing that you are not clever enough or not pretty enough, or not interesting enough, so you will retreat and isolate yourself from socializing - all leading to more serious issues and severe insecurities and fears. All these convictions are false and taught, while representing an extension of your parent. You can change your distorted cognition by relying on facts and truth. Whenever you are in doubt and whenever you are not sure whether your thoughts and assumptions are based on facts or are just the side effect of distorted cognition, you should try to actualize your own thoughts and check the validity of the way you think. For example, if you think that you are not clever enough, you need to prove it to yourself with only using facts and pure logic as if you are observing yourself from someone else's perspective. As long as you keep your facts in line and use objectivity and logic, you can question your own cognition and determine which of your convictions represent false logic – that way you will be able to discover your true qualities and traits without relying on your fears and doubts. When you are able to separate negative thoughts developed through false cognition from reality and facts, you will be able to fight insecurities and fears as a product of imagined reality where extremes rule. You need to become aware of the fact that your parent's cognition found its way to you as you were exposed to the devastating effects of growing up with a parent who cannot come up with appropriate emotional and behavioral responses – but you shouldn't allow your past to stop you from reimagining your identity and developing your sense of self. Make sure to rely on facts in order to avoid false convictions and acting upon distorted cognition.

#23 Find Your Courage

It takes courage to make a change and since you are already here and have come so far, we can already tell that you have the courage it takes – you just might not be aware of your strengths as you've never gained any form of recognition from your parent. You may not know it yet, but it also takes courage to survive neglect and lack of affirmation, affection, recognition and negative psychosocial models – you have the courage it takes and it is time for you to realize that statement as a fact. You are still here, you are still standing, you are still fighting and you are not giving up – the mere fact that you are looking for a solution shows your readiness to accept new changes as well as motivation to change for better. Regardless of the fact that some bad things require no right or reason in order to happen, you have the courage to face any case scenario as you are still here and aware that there is a problem in your life that needs to be resolved. What you might be lacking is a positive affirmation and we are here to remind you that you can achieve any goal you set before yourself. This is not an empty pep-talk – this is a reminder of who you are and of who you seek to become. Relieve your fears and doubts and try understanding that there isn't any form of punishment waiting for you in case you make a mistake or experience a setback. Relax and have faith in yourself and the courage you have yet to discover deep within you. Test your courage by trying to do something simple that otherwise makes you feel uncomfortable and that usually triggers a form of fear, doubt or anxiety. For example, if you have been invited to a party by one of your friends or your acquittance and you came up with an excuse why you are unable to attend the party out of fear when you actually wanted to go, have a change of heart and accept the invitation. Any fear or doubt that might convince you that you are boring or not interesting enough, should be left out from the equation. If you need confirmation that you are "good enough", use facts instead of diving into your fears and doubts.

#24 Motivate Yourself

Motivation is the main key towards achieving a positive change. A change cannot be forced upon you the way your parent imposed their own perception of the world on you. You need to say YES to a positive change and motivate yourself into truly accepting your past and the fact that you are willing to leave the past behind while only using past experiences as lessons that will help you to facilitate a positive change and develop your own identity of which you were deprived in the early years of your life. As a child, you might not had many options, but as an adult who is aware of everything negative that happened to you, you have a choice to change your perspective and live a happier and more fulfilling life where you are free to enjoy beautiful things and ready to accept that sometimes bad things just happen, and that is what life is in the end. Motivate yourself into completing your path of change even if it appears that you are not able to and that you can't go on. You can, only if you truly wish to – it just takes will and effort. You can personalize the way you are motivating yourself and come up with a way that will help you move on and keep going even when it appears that you can't go on.

#25 Set Realistic Goals for Your Own Future

Try not to go ahead of yourself when setting goals for the future – you might be used to fulfilling unreal and illogical expectations imposed by your parent, but that doesn't mean that you should push yourself too hard, especially in the beginning as you are only starting to adapt to a new life you want to create for yourself. Start with setting up simple and smaller goals for yourself regarding your future. For instance, you can start with coming up with ways to get involved in a creative or relieving hobby, so you can start with cooking classes or join a reading club where you can practice your confidence and social interaction, that way gaining more perks from a single activity. Hobbies are an excellent way to start with smaller achievements that will encourage you to set more serious and bigger goals. Perhaps you wish to improve your expertise and finish college or sign up for master studies and grow personally and professionally, or maybe you are looking for an opportunity to start your own business or find a job that would make you happy at the end of the weekend. Whichever your goals are for the future, you should list them all and work on achieving them – however, you should avoid criticizing yourself when things aren't going that smooth, and neither should you consider giving up when you encounter difficulties. As we mentioned before in the guide, both good things and bad things represent a normal part of life. After all, being happy all the time doesn't make sense as much as being sad all the time doesn't make a life. You will use facts once again to trace and list your goals together with your inclinations, wishes, traits, qualities and talents, and you will use everything you have at your disposal to gradually achieve your goals. Good things take time, remember. You also need to make sure to give praise to yourself whenever a goal from your list is achieved, regardless of how small and insignificant this achievement may appear to you. There are no insignificant achievements if you manage to complete any of the goals you set before you.

#26 Live in the Present, Make Peace with Traumatic Past

It can be very difficult to leave the past behind, especially when your past has affected your present life and current state of mind. In order to reestablish your identity, you need to make peace with your traumatic past and understand that your childhood doesn't have to define your adulthood and the rest of your life. As we mentioned before, life is consisted of bad and good things, and sometimes bad things just happen – even to good people. As soon as you realize that sometimes bad things happen even to people that don't deserve it, it will be easier for you to make peace with a traumatic part of your life and allow yourself to move on and get over what you have been through. This can be achieved by forgiving yourself and forgiving others that might have caused you pain. That way you are showing that you do not allow your past to define who you are today. To make this process easier, you can try gradually making peace by living in the present. Every new morning is a new chance for you to shine and try making your life better, so you should try starting fresh every day even if the last day could have been better. This technique will help you with focusing on the present and experiencing new moments and events that are happening in the present. You cannot control the future, and you can't change the past, but you can live in the present and try making every day count.

#27 Forgive

Although you probably think that we are suggesting that you should forgive your parent, we are actually urging you to forgive yourself. You are most probably taking all the blame for what is happening to you and what has been happening to you in your past. The chances are that you are also taking blame for other negative things happening to other people even if it is not you who had caused their misfortunes. Ask yourself for forgiveness and give yourself forgiveness. It is natural that you might have the need to forgive your parents as well – and just as we have urged you to forgive yourself, we are strongly advising that you forgive your parents for causing you pain by not realizing that they projected their problems onto you – their child. You don't have to face your parents and say that you forgive them – while the chances are that your parent is not even aware of the fact that they should be asking for your forgiveness. You can do that silently in your own mind once you feel ready to make peace with your past. Forgiveness will provide you with a chance to resolve a problematic chapter in your life and stop it from defining you in the present.

#28 Know Yourself - Separate Yourself from Negative Influences

Just as you are not defined by your trauma, you are also not defined by the negative influences you have suffered. Due to the fact that you have grown up under these negative influences transferred to you by your NPD or BPD parent with an untreated condition, you may have a difficult time separating your identity from the negative influences you were exposed to in fragile years of development. This is a step you can't miss on taking as you need to analyze your characteristics, your emotions and your behavior patterns – list them in a diary if it easier for you to follow up with key metrics this way – and decide which one of these belong to you and which were implemented and forced upon you during your bringing up. Once again, you will use facts to find out which emotions are yours and which represent side effects from traumatic experiences in your childhood and adolescence.

That way you will be certain of which traits you should keep and work on and which characteristics should be gradually removed from your thoughts, emotional responses and behavior patterns. By changing your habits, furthermore, and by changing your mindset to a more positive stance, you should be able to enjoy your present and look forward to the future without evoking emotional turmoil every time your childhood is brought up or thought of.

#29 Relieve Negative Emotions and Thoughts

Release all negativity to free your mind – analyze your thoughts whenever you are able to notice that you are jumping to negative conclusions or imagining worst case scenarios, while also assuming what people think about you. Whenever you are able to note that some of these thoughts are evoking negative emotions or enticing negative behavior patterns, you can make a pause and do a quick analysis by using FACTS. Facts are going to become your new best friends as it will represent your anchor of sense and logic whenever you are in doubt. By relieving negative thoughts, you should be able to change the way you are experiencing emotions when in distress, while also being able to change negative behavior patterns. Letting go of past will help you let go of emotional turmoil and negative thoughts, consequently leading to reestablishing your own self with an improve and REALISTIC image of yourself.

#30 Live Your Own Life

It is your God-given right to live your life the way you want to and in accordance with your own sense of self and your own individuality and values, in oppose to living a life imposed by your neglecting and perhaps abusive parent.

You are not a villain, even though your parent probably managed to convince you into taking blame for their sadness, depression, fears and anxiety. Remember, the world is not all black and white although your parent tried their hardest to convince you into believing in extremes as a part of their own perception. Take off the glasses of darkness and see the light that your life represents. Your life is your own and it doesn't belong to anyone else, so you are the only one entitled to decide what to do with it and how to make the best out of the life you have. Believing that you are born to satisfy other people's needs, take care of everyone and anyone on the cost of your happiness, and fulfill unrealistic requirements and needs imposed by your parent are all the things that will keep you stuck between what you feel you need to do and what you wish you had courage to do. Don't blame your parents either – or yourself – accept the fact that you have been through a series of traumatic experiences and influences, and that you can now move onto living your life to the fullest. Happiness is freedom, and freedom means living a happy life without looking back and feeling regret for things you couldn't possibly control.

Conclusion

Your journey guided by our book might have ended, but you have a long way ahead of you – a way of new opportunities and self-recognitions. Remember to love yourself, respect yourself and appreciate yourself with at least the same intensity you appreciate other people and their own individualities. Remember that every new morning means a new opportunity, while what you make of your present will define a better future - not your past. Let go of your traumatic experiences and leave the past where it belongs. You can return to our guide whenever you are in doubt or need support on your journey towards resolving your past traumas from being raised by parents who were unfortunately driven by their mental condition left untreated. Take the best out of every day, take risks and chances, and give yourself the respect you deserve.

Did We Help?

We care about our readers, so naturally we consider your opinion to be the most valuable measure for the quality of our content. Our guides and books are written based on careful research and expertise and are due to provide help for those in need. We appreciate your opinion and your attention, and we try to live up to our readers' expectations by offering viable solutions set to help people and guide them through a problem based on careful research, so we would likewise appreciate if you would make your opinion on our book public. If we managed to help and offer solutions in a comprehensive way, and in case you found our material more than helpful, please share your rating with others and let us know how we managed to help!

Happy to help and offer our practical knowledge,

Thank you!

www.ingramcontent.com/pod-product-compliance
Lightning Source LLC
Chambersburg PA
CBHW050212270326
41914CB00003BA/372